SILENCE ATTACK

GODA ANDRULIONYTE

DEDICATION

My parents
Collin & Justin
Alexander Zarach
Benedict Green

CONTENTS
Acknowledgments

ix

x

1 *Chemical*

Cautious trumpets
Play in the background
Within the cafe full of hippies

Hippies consuming chemicals
Nature vs. Nurture

Freshly picked mushrooms
Scattered on the ground
Illusions enjoyed by the thirsty
Taking away into enchanted places
Green trees turned into blue
The biochemical has worked well

Underachieving teenagers
Play in white powder
Surrounded by crime
Forgetting their morals
Empowered by contagious feelings of heaven
Where are they?

2 *Valleys*

The bread I've once swallowed
Leaves a tasteless taste
In the middle of my mouth
Dictating my stream of adrenalin

Purified madness
Feasting upon my senses
Concluding in unmistakable
Expressions of happiness

Unforgettable heat
Draining the flesh
Of cold bodies

Broken glass
Scattered on the ground
Leading to valleys
That once belonged to God

Forests of fear
Surround the valley
Of glass

Cold bodies
Once used to dine
In the darkened forest

Madness foolishly contaminate
The children of the king
Leaving heat to its job
Never again

Bread served
For the homeless,
Migrants of the valley
Competing against the rich
With beer to the left
And wine to the right

3 *Riches*

Hipsters
Running around
Naked
Nature whipping their butts
Torturing their souls
Reminding them of their views
Failing to differentiate the century
They cry in their pads

The riches
Screaming at the powerless
Forgetting their on species
Flourished in white powder
Pushed into gullible existence
Pursuing their lives of darkened misery
Disguised in financial crushes

Who wants to be the richest corpse in the graveyard?

4 *Petals*

Petals glow
Stems are steep
The summer weather
A fool's season

Petals gone
Shrunk stems
Down under the ground
Burning in sorrow
For our lives
Our happiness
Autumn, the wise man's season

5 Demolition

Woods of fear
Persuading a magical dance
To grip your arm and
Take you inside
The house of demolition

Scattered ashes on the ground
Temperatures beyond imagination
Experiences of which nobody cares for

The stench of dead mammals
Layer the walls
Like the Pacific Ocean
Full of ashes
From the house of demolition

6 *Comprehension*

I'm never sad
I'm too happy
Beyond your comprehension

I write like I'm dead
Yet meanings beyond our dimension

Understand me
If you try
A glimpse of my imagination
Is simply not enough

A ride through my thoughts
Is beyond all possibilities

Products of dairy
Will never help
It runs through the stars
In the morning light
That's the only way to comprehend

7 Miracles

Cinderella
Was a princess
Perhaps a queen

Yet she was a slave
She barged through misery,
On dark roads

Her deeds were good,
Yet she never understood,
She thought it was it,
Then she faced a miracle

One we shall never experience.
It simply doesn't exist.
Every girl waits for it,
Finding nothing,
And die.

I guess that's a girl's life...

8 *Past*

Flying through Streets,
I look toward the end of the path.
I remember myself,
My history,
My future.

It is blank.
Like a sheet of unrolled pastry.

It is blank.
But built up my spirit,
Personality,
Mood.

I had no one.
Just a slim blow of air,
Flowing past my ears,
Slapping my pale cheeks.

Everyone turned against me.

The floor was cold,
Always.

9 Illusions

Beautiful girls,
Swirling around the world,
Looking for a place to hide their feelings.

Men of pure heart searching for the most beautiful,
Forgetting their hearts full of hatred,
If they're lucky they will find,
If not they will fall in a well,
In a well called love.

This well darkens as you fall deeper,
Deeper into the districts of pain.

It starts of contredingly,
Yet you are still falling,
Ends up with a huge bump to the back,
Cracking each bone in your body.

Don't fall down the well.

10 *Worries*

Drunken birds,
All around my porch,
Sing their lullaby,
Each on different,
Forming natures orchestra.

Children running,
Place to place,
No one is worried,
But their mothers,
Mothers which are still alive.

Preachers preaching,
The wonders of our dreams,
Slowly swallowing,
Our valid feelings,
Throwing them away,
Into the dark.

11 Happiness

I'm always happy,
Yet there's no booze in my hand.

I'm always proud,
Yet drugs are never seen.

Music.

Music is my answer.
It takes me away,
Away
To Places I can be happy and proud of.

I am the soul in my heart.

Music is the leader to my heart.

12 Try

I sit in the middle of my room,
Day after day.

Wondering where I lead myself.
What if I'm the drunken hobo?
You saw the other day?

What if, I'm the lawyer everyone,
Goes to for help and advice.

I try my best,
Achieve average,
Average?
Average is not enough.
I must work harder.

Until I die of a brain tumor.
Sitting, In the middle of my mind.

13 *Life and its expectations*

Each day,
I am judged.

In the most unexpected forms
I am called weird
A hippie
Hipster
Too happy
Ugly
Spot face

I grow to accept these?
But I thought you said life
Is a fun rollercoaster...?

You're wrong

14 Life and death

I've never lost a person in my life
Only dogs
Maybe cats
But animals aren't that much of a hassle

Life brings us many expectations
We go to many strange places
We see, hear, feel and smell things
Things we may either regret
Or applaud

Death plays the opposite role
Death locks us up
In an odd dark cage
We do not move
We just stay
In one place

We are locked away from dreams
For all eternity

15 *Power*

If I were a boy
I'd feast on many

Girls would run
And others would sacrifice

All power would be claimed
All would be damned

The king would conquer
Your land and your life

But I'm just a girl
I'm weak, terrified of grief

Insecure

Troubled

Stupid

If only I were a boy...

17 *Born too late*

I was late for the excitement of Jazz
Mostly for the two exquisite writers - Alan and Jack

I'm too late to experience the end of the cold war
I'm way too late
For the rival of the hippies

I'm just born too late

I'm in the generation of boredom
Where even the rich and the poor
Can afford phones

I see the idiots act out their beliefs
I am stereotyped as the 'bad kid'
Thanks to the others

I am expected to have no dignity
Like the girls of Geordie Shore

But I'm the opposite
I live a life of non-stop Jazz
I am swept away by Jack and Allan

18 *Dear ol' friend*

When I listen to myself
I hear my best friend
This friend of mine, I trust
Not something you can do with others

This friend understands me
My parents have no hope for us both
People never notice us together
Yet they know we are together

I dearly love my true friend

More than a boyfriend

More than parents

More than anything

She speaks to me day/night
Not every friend would do the same

We care...
Care?
No, we have none of that
Apart for our well-being, but nothing else

19 *Everyday*

Everyday
I walk a path
In which I meet failure and success
In which I feel despair and utter happiness

With failure, comes despair
It eats up every part of your body
It manipulates my thoughts with anguish
Utter disappointment

With success, comes light
It brings me pure adrenalin
I see the light, as if I own it
The abolishment of neediness is final
Most of all?
Insecurity strikes
But I like it this way...

20 Hopelessness

Factors influencing my life
Projecting my feelings
Affiliating my fears

Sandstorms attacking cities
Puncturing holes
In windows and buildings

Angry people
Complaining in anguish
From past to present

Birds showing of their feathers
Stealing the strongest
Kidnaping attention

Assumptions to backstabbing's
Alliteration killing the suspense

Murder accomplished
Loss in blood of others

Dreams cannot descend

21 *Mother nature*

Why the sad smile?
You're known for your seductive one
Everyone knows you're not sad
Just stop it, ok?

Do you see that tree?
The one with its leaves
Annihilated from the ugly trunk
By the will of Mother Nature
Yes
That's what you remind me of

Mother Nature is a bit of an ass, though
It's as if she intoxicates herself
The good parts are on the beautiful people and places
The bad parts
That comes on the hangover
Are on the ugly people and places
It's obvious her hangovers are more frequent
Just look at you

22 A better world

Imagine
Imagine a world without music
A world without overdoses of movement
A world, full of idiotic imbeciles

Stress
Stressed prostitutes
Pushing around
Charging low fees, for hungry impassioned men
Just to hear them
Just for the sake,
Of an overdose of movement and sound

Depression
Depression strikes
Everyone hates one another
Prostitutes killing themselves
Just for the sake
Of a better life
Of a better world

23 Taking over our lives

Plaguematic research
Affiliate our minds
Our senses
Our morals

Industries blinding pigeons
Many circulating through systems
Rather than blood circulating our heads

Death rates increasing
Governments partying
Evaluating our lives
As if we were clones

Robots created
Stealing our minds
Hacking our feelings
Replacing with drugs

Plaguematic research
Taking over our lives

24 *Heavenly feathers*

Royal dances
Performed for the king
Pretentious vibes of love
Portray an atmosphere of imprecise hatred

The soft breeze outside
Control the petals on branches
Pink from the Nature of spring

Spirals
Leading to drawing rooms
Covered in gold
From generations long passed to Heaven

Feather from silk cushions
Devour a room
Where the innocent slumber

Calm mornings
Inspired by ponderous
Classical Jazz

Empty rooms

Devoured
In light colors
Pink Green Blue

Immaculate personalities
Surrender
To en noir et blanc
Paintings
From considerate artists

We all rest
In cautious conspiracy

25 Natures openings

End of another day
I walk the usual path
The red path

The trees surround me
Side by side
With the swaying of leaves
Songs of birds
And Jazz on my iPod
I remember

I remember
My secrets, which don't exist
My happiness, which I always hide
My feelings, which are always annotated by others

The sky is mild blue
Splashes of white clouds
I forget
The madness in my head

26 *Popularity*

Flawless cheeks
Of red rose beauties,
Walk the world
Are told the false truth
By jealous creatures

Long noses
Patrol a city of industry

Outrageous hats
Assumed as fashion
Worn by the royal
Dumped by the realists
Retrieved by the artists

Rhythmic drumming
Silence the natives
Reform the lovers

Hearts racing
Towards the finals
The last a winner
Receiving time

Paper flowing
Used for intelligence

Scraped away
When overused

Couples dancing
To streetlights flashing
Sleeping above,
Waving at the unintelligent

Mainstream singers singing
Grabbing money
From the majority
Art forgotten
Ignored by the popular
Caressed by le inimitable

Attraction renforcee

27 Truths Held In Life

I never wear skirts
It shows my false identity
Trousers and shorts,
Rule over my choices
Didn't your God once say,
Attachment is a sin

A vase of flowers
Accomplishes the decorations in my room
Apparently Black, Red and White
Is simply not enough

I get along better with the elder
They've had a long life
Understanding things
I will fail to accomplish

A different generation
The modern – worthless
Yet I guess every generation was the same
Every

28 *Fire*

Roaring flames
Take over our Oxygen
Covering land in Carbon
Hazard masks are doomed

Screeches surround Villages
Running through alleyways
Full of Methane

Neighbors gone
Trapped in the skies of wonder

 Beauty emerged flowers
Melt in high temperatures
Life underneath
Gone in a snap

Carbonated bones
Layer floors of Cement

Schools shut down
Open to the Devils children

Mountains
Once surrounded in ice
Scrapped naked in a second
Unable to hide the expensive inside

Another world unpopulated
Turned into another star

The Devils playground

29 *Morning*

Waking up
It's 5:29am
Only five hours of sleep
What on Earth am I doing?

Anne Frank's diary
Lies on the other side of the coach
Turn to page one
Oh! An introduction!

My mother's awake?
But it's only 7:01am

The kitchen's a mess
What can I do?
Rubbish bin isn't too full
Thank God

Sister's here
But It's only 8:05a!
Making noise
With the Fire Truck toy

30 *Springs Spirit*

Flowers growing
Color reendowed
By Nature's own wish

Everyone is outside
Even me
I doubt this is permanent

Slaughtered pig's
Would you prefer Halal?
The smell of burnt Barbecue
I'm not hungry
She is

Fried Chicken?
Nope
Not served anymore

It's Monday!
Bank holiday
Oh no!
I'm suddenly depressed

Massive Attack

Play on my laptop
Group four
She melts my soul
Shit!
I don't exist

Nerds
Locked up at home
I'm one of them
Today's my break though
Oh well
It's Monday

31 *Jazz lights*

Sparkle, sparkle
Dresses made of silk
Corrupted in diamonds

Girls and boys
Dance their hopes away

Lighters
Used to light cigars
Now set fire to hair

Trumpets play
Girls and boys
With love
And hatred in the other

Piano's dance
In the spotlight
The handsome man
Every man's jealous
Oh, the calamity!

Attraction
Set's this place to fire

I'm afraid it's too old
To outstand 1000 fans

Steak is served
Nobody cares
Wine is served!
Everyone runs

Oh my God!
A 'couple' making out
Tomorrow
They'll say goodbye

Cruises dismissed
I forgot my luggage
You've got to be kidding me...

32 Dark Street

Shadows on the ground
Force me to stop and turn
Figures I've never encountered
Stare into my flesh

Streetlamps
Force light onto my head
But the dark wins over my body
Using it for clothing and meat

I encounter a strange fox
It looks at me with its sinister grin
I cannot move
Yet I fear that if I stay
I die

The man with the glasses
Wins over my eyesight
My smile
I follow him home
I feel, somewhat inspired
His posture, face

We enter a pitch black tunnel
Bewitched by darkness

Black
Dark
Black
Dark

I do not stop
My footsteps hypnotize my moves
Tip
Top
Tip
Top

I begin to lose control
I close my eyes
Still follow the man

I stop

I am conscious
I open my eyes
Trees
Water
Trees
Water

My arm is aggressively grabbed
My soul descends into a war over life
My shadow moved away
Parting the body

Suddenly
I am alive

33 *Dirty feet*

I walk the farm
Once again
Feet are bare
Hands are clean

Sun is setting
Pulling the kids to bed

Wolves Howl
Chanting their lifeless prayers

The air is full of scent
Mixed with Roses and Lavender

Few houses surround me
Each with their lights out
Each person inside fast asleep

The hay is soft
Yet the floor is rough
My beer is cold
My feet are warm

My music is the wind
Blowing past my hair and body
My eyelids hide my eyes
From Natures harsh capabilities

My house is empty
I live alone
I face my fears alone

I see a bird
Which bird, I do not know
It fly's in circles
Circulating my spirit
It slowly lowers toward my Left shoulder

I walk with a bird

34 *Bonjour*

I look outside the window
It's so huge
I can sit on its window bay
Without a struggle

The people pass my sight
Without a single hello

The flowers outside
Change the view, completely
From basic marble and brick
To colorful land of heaven

A small French girl
Strides across the pavement
Her dress
Flourished in pink and white
Volume added from the material underneath

She catches my eye
Shouting Bonjour Mademoiselle

I shall never forget

35 *Wild child*

She runs past mad inquires
Sticking her middle finger
To the ones who disagree

She succeeds at attempting her vigorous tricks
Losing many
Who hoped for a spirit I her heart

She grabs money of counters
Hiding in rubbish cans
On our parks

Shouting her name
Striking fear
In the middle of Texas

Many worshiped
Terrified of her gun

She was a wild girl

36 Lotus cherry

A pond
Surrounded in Natures beauty

Green frogs
Lay on leaves
In the center of this pond

The transparent water
Clear enough
For its nature to be widely seen

The fish inside
Sworn past the Lotus in the pond

Daytime
The sacred light
Of the pink Lotus
Compelling astonishment
Of passing animals

A cherry tree
Covering the light
Creating a dark side
To the Lotus pond

Birds' nests
Rest in the cherry tree

Cherries
Flaunting the land
In sweet nectre of pureness
A cherry tree
A life giver

A pink Lotus
The souls inner peace

37 Misty fragrance

The land of water
Full of creatures
Oil on its head
Along with boats of all kind

Cruises
Never empty
Taking the adventurous
On a journey through our world

That room
Surrounded in antiques
Unique
With its misty fragrance

The fragrance
Catches both man and women
Controlling mood
From hot to cold

Sensitivity arising
Bullying their senses
Taking them to sleep
One by one...

38 *Blood on my floor*

The door is shut
Along with the window
A one room apartment
I used to live here

Red splashes
On the dirty white walls
Left and right
This place isn't big

A black knife
Dropped on my stone floor
Now turned red
I don't sleep in here

Curtains ripped
Onto my red floor
Drenched in blood
No, I did not drop my
Red, red wine

Feet Drenched in blood
I look outside my small window
Grabbing my small window bay
Lights surround this council

Feet drenched in blood
I didn't do it, Sir

39 *Put down the wine*

Sitting on my black coach
We discuss this problem
With 5 bottles on my table

This place is cold
Yet too hot for you
This place is too bright
I hate the light
It bottles up my senses
Abolishing my imagination

I am insecure
Exactly why I'm not drunk
I already have the excitement
Passing through my body
Alcohol kills it

My personality
It is cold
Yet nobody complains

Instead, everyone loves

I take another sip,
Of this cheap wine
I must admit
It lightens up my soul
From complete darkness
To somewhat holy heaven

Oh no!
Help me
I'm on my second glass
Tired
What's in this thing?
I won't stop drinking
My taste bugs beg for more

You try to discourage me
Never going to work
My mind,
Is locked up in the spirals of distress

This world will kill me
It's too complicated
I'm too weak,
My friend

40 *Vine Leaves*

The Gods fruit
Decorate,
The back garden,
Of my house

Never trimmed –
They cannot be!
Left to grow
In all its wish
To never be bothered
In its solemn habitat

It grows like crazy
Covering half of my house
Growing into the house
From my windows and doors

The fruit is never ripe
Always tiny and green
Not touched
By its owners
The humans themselves

Letting out a sweet glow
In the summer time season
Dropping its leaves
In the autumn and winter

Now it is spring
Slowly regaining
Its leftover spirit
Storing new food
For our Gods,
In heaven and hell

Sitting in the garden
Enjoying the view,
Of nature herself

Ripe strawberries
Can never over rule it

The holy Vine leaves...

41 *Black Clouds*

Loud storms
Threaten the youngsters
Frighten the older
Swipe away the sensitive

Calm shores
Are aggravated
Swaying past helpless towns
Innocent surrendering their worth
Their life

Televisions portraying the consequences
From America
To China

Who is to be blamed?
For such agony

Dead bodies
Layer Oceans
Black clouds
Travel to another...

42 *Broken Stem*

Fields, full of glory
Conquer the land of the living
The spread of heavens own scent
Brings light to the mood of a wife

Picking many
For sale, then for death
Meeting the trash can
Is never a good sign

One brought
By one man
Taking care
For its broken stem
Remembering its original state

Children full of ponder
Grab another stem
Taking one for games
Disposing in a pin drop

A married woman

Coming home
To a magical scent,
Of fields and green forests

Yielding to its power
Smelling from above
Enjoying the nostril buzz
Vanquish of distress

A husband coming home
To a woman's smile
Describing her intense pleasure
Forgiving his past deeds

The power of a broken stem
The secret to a perfect marriage...

43 *White Swan*

Blue lakes
Covered in live animals
From insects and mammals
Swerving past bacteria

Humans invading
Nature's territory
Trashing the lake
From sandwiches to trollies

Green stuff
Flowing above the water
Providing the tiny with food
Councils removing
For the sake of our sight

A white swan
Swimming by
With babies behind
Acting as followers
The future dancers
In the lake of life

The children stare
Admiring the feathers
Wishing as a pet
Begging for its company up close

Elders, throwing bread
Remembering the gay memories
Disapproving of the worse
Leaving the negative for last

Teenage girls, dreaming
Of future husbands holding their hand
Walking the pathway of pure harmony
Enhanced by the white bird
Fantasizing of a white dress

The swan
A spell on all…

44 Violet Silk

With a scarf around my shoulders
An arm wrapped around my back
I walk into the live night

Classical Opera
Silence the crowd
Second by second

Gentlemen each married
Leaving their thoughts of the attractive artist behind
After all
It is a sin
To love another

Her opera dress shimmers
Shimmers more than any others'
Her father the provider

Unmarried,
The Church deceives her

Friends are jealous

The men only pay attention to the elegant

Her red cheeks
Pale white skin
Ginger hair
Black teeth
Large eyes
No one can copy

She reaches out,
To no religious belief
The Ten Commandments are of no matter to the lady

The voice of an angel
Collide with thought of the Devil
Secrets kept
Her mind kept shut from the public
After all
The witch can never reveal her identity

Her dress of violet silk
Shimmers in the light
Colorless in the night

45 *Rose Wine*

The rain, pouring down
I hear it on my window
Clear of wind
Buckets of water

Bed undone
I lay and write all day
There's nothing better to do

You look into my face
Spotting a tear
Your face wears a rigid expression

To let you know
It's not your fault

The printer is on
What should I print?
Images of my eye?

A glass on my table
Empty

No more Wine left
I want some more…

I'm bored?
I'm boring

The cries of my sister
Make her stop!!

The smell of food
I don't want any

My friend's becoming Bulimic
I can only stare in pity
She never listens
Media's finally reached her mind set

I stare at my laptop
Lifeless
I wish I knew how to spend time outside…

46 *Empty Fields*

Running away
The houses pass me like the air
Cars, controlled by angry men
Continue to beep their horns

Acceleration increasing
Unable to look back
When did I turn toward the wrong angle?

Friends waving
When did I first wave hello?

Hearts crushed
Oh, the fun teenage years

Passing a knife
It almost touched me!
I took it myself
Thank God I dropped it

Meditation
So hard to learn
So hard to forget

Karma,
Led me to fields of fear
Karma,
Led me to fields of joy

Knowledge,
Led me to misty forts
The pen,
Led me to neutrality

An empty field
Beautiful,
For the things it contains

Empty fields,
Where I plan on sleeping tonight

Empty fields,
Where I plan to die...

47 *I am not alive*

Sitting under the apple tree
Letting go of its leaves
Through my soul
To the ground

Looking across the forest
To the blonde headed figure

A light breeze
Follow my sight
Pursuing to blow apples on my head

An Adirondack style house
The place I hid our existence
The place we drank our wine

A river in the far left
The place we fell in love
The place we fell for greed

The sun is gone
It's an American night

Moonlight is fierce
Yet still,
The forest is dark

She's still there
Facing the Jeep
Showing of her pale back

Hands are raised
Where has she gone?

48 White magic

The brand new penthouse
The top of Italy
Where new life is deemed to exist

Sailors,
Walking the shallow shores
Back and forth
Longing for a new ship to sail

Bouts of Brighton
Rule the piers or Rome
The smell of drugs
Faint, but real

Policemen,
Searching bodies
Looking for wands
That overrules death
Unable to decide
Where to dispose

The city lights

Masking our holy city
Patrolling the chemicals
Disguised as tourists to life
From cities long behind

Monuments,
Built long ago
By our almighty ancestors
That used to pray for our Capitalized land

Birds,
Searching our city
Fed by our holy priests
Thin, in the body and mind

Running late
Your cab vanished
Away to another
Your job is too fragile,
Buy a car
Poor ole friend

49 *Colorless balloons*

Floating in the air
The helium so light,
Heavy in our hands

Wind,
The almighty controller
Leading a masterpiece
Around our sky's
To the mountains of our dreams

Look above,
Color may never seem the same
As the sight toward tomorrow

Look past mans' skyscrapers,
You shall observe much more
Drain the details
Into the unconscious mind
Sleep with nightmares
Of heaven above reality

Trigger misery away,

Nightmares are no excuse

Apologize to the rich,
They think they've all the best
Yet blindness preaches their dreams

Present yourself with laughter
Joy will take your hand,
Onto the journey you presumed a lie

Balloons devour a room
How sweet the colors are
They paint throughout
From ceiling to ground
Oh, how I wish, a ballroom of color

Nights in Venice,
An angels land in love
Couples kissing,
Portraying their feelings
Through holding hands
And swaying in wooden bouts

Oh how I wish,
A world so light

50 *You too?*

The lanes heath
The time caught your eyes
The special wand was brought to life

Cigarettes in our mouths
The smoke so grey,
I can barely see your face
The dark stench,
Penetrating our brain cells
Yet everything was clear,
Too clear

You pushed my mind into your dish,
Eating every part
As if you owned another

Light dimmed
From my pale, dark face
You too, took another life

Live with her,
But with my memory inherited
Dismiss your soul

51 Wildflowers

Turn to a light destination
Persuade your senses into distress
Annihilate all possibilities of pleasure
Stay in the arms of several dark angels
Portray a speeding red light into eyes of dark preachers
Pick a brown leaf
Place into a shallow river
Watch it sink to the bottom of its life
Sicken your peers, into believing your dark lies
Grow up in crime and hatred
Negativity will never reach your mouth
Or as an angel once spoke into your ear
Forget all goodness or banish in societies torture
Disengage from all the rules you've followed
Build a house of sand
Live under pitch black walls
Surrender to gloom and schizoid madness
Eat nothing but fish
Drink all but water
Destroy all feeling of harmony
Inherit heart aches for pudding
Push yourself into deaths stove
Wake up in my arms…

52 A Dreams Feather

Caress another living soul,
The timid ache, inside a heart,
Is never the same
When eyesight is drawn, toward the enticing
body of resign

A rushed pulse
Swaying mind to a land of seduction
Igniting the fuel of emotions
Obliging the dreamland itself

Strut another night away
Same soul throwing passion to your mind
Faith is high
No one here,
But the fierce seducer
Slender eyes
Convoying your senses

Throw away the flowers of abstruse daylight

Blossomed trees
Capture pulchritude in your eyes
The glimpse of one,
Nights of life for you

Open your clenched fists
Feel the elegant air,
Of the feather you've feared of holding

A bewitched flower,
Alone in forests of peculiar beings,
Found by the wrong
Trampled by the right

Figures blemishing in toxic waste
Enduring in poison atmosphere

Corrosive metals spoil tender sights
The harsh reaction
Clenching our minds
The mists grab
The feeling of your desperate heart

53 Summer Garden

Birds of numerous creations
Rule the porch of blue and green

Savior pond,
The dirty green liquid
A sight enjoyed by fish of splendiferous glint

Jewels of beckoning praises
Surround the porch seat
In which a young female may devour her rest

Cold blooded insects
Prey on the gardens lavish scene

A mixture of divine surroundings
A walk through color
Surprisingly a damned illusion kept far apart from life

Pets of neighbors
Contaminate a garden of their territory
Remark of honest greatness
Feast on red meat and white milk

National liquor
Brought in for longing parties
Joy to the greedy
Fear for the hopeful

Worn out shoes
In orange light panic
Embrace a rigid texture
To front doors and dirty feet

Linger toward dead trees
Presume a fantasy of clear blue skies

Puncture past a garden wall
Enjoy a bragging reunion of clamorous friends
Loud and harsh
Yet all is fine as thread in needle

Remember to mark an old man's words
For you may be last
In the garden of pure pretense beauty

54 A flowing Gesture

Passing through a sea of time
The weather descends to a maniacs scarf

Each child home in safe hearts
With doors and windows sealed in pride
Nothing to fear,
But the monster above their sacred heads

A free bird
Fleeing to its nurtured nest
For tonight is a night,
Of mammals and ghosts

The gardener's chair,
Free to the warm rain
Comfortable and pampered
For the foxes coming by

The pass of nights' fog
The smell of trapped firewood,
In the air that's roams our nightmares
Tense in fashion
Blank in taste of cigarettes

A kiss,
Laced upon her pale blue lips
She's waited hours and hours,
Before the figure of her dreams
Would love her like the Cupids child

The men of artistic hatred
Will stay in sight another night
His darkened hands will wave goodnight
By daylights touch to Earth's soul

55 *Brainwashed*

A stream of false beliefs
Told by idiots in mind – numbing captivity
Yet genius in the deep end of lies

The purely white beards
Lost a thousand years ago
Returns to please a thousand minds
The texture deep
In wool and cotton

The land in which an animal lays lifeless
Left to men of cold hearts
Abused by industry and politics
Society using for their pleasure
Nature dying in the hands of man

The outdoor smell
Pollution over roses
The wicked wizard has returned

The tears of innocent
Ignored by inhumane enemies
Wasting time on their guilty thoughts

56 *Seedless Territory*

Strong minded
Fellow beings
Live in a very merry place

No grass in sight
No tree in view
Sculptures and buildings
Take over your eye

Cars roam,
In fashionable pride
Mans' treasure
Disguised in steel and fabric

A maze of Iron
Made for the lost
To be found in traffic

Petrified under white walls
Too light for a soul of dark aura

Mortified wives
Observe the immoral,

Yet act as blinded birds
Preached gently by mentally wounded husbands

A red light
Directed into the forehead
Enticed toward the delivering senses
Shone out,
Toward primary reactions

Life is viewed as pleasuring existence
Sent to dissembled asylums
If viewed from the wrong direction

Merrily blessed
A priests longing sin made
Who is there to listen to his lies now?

57 *Prudence Guilt*

Nude shores
Over masculine Nations
Enjoyed by the food of man
Too cold for man himself

The peach tree
Sunlight penetrates its leaves
Losing its beauty
Blossom far from appearance

Grass green,
Yet growing dry
By every step of your way

A hand gun on a table
Used several times,
Yet never caught
By another living man

The white powder
You call it a warrior of your life
Ignoring the pain

You survive another hour

Daylight shone
Into another pair of miserable eyes
Another precious life
Prepared for new lies

Persecution is too simple,
For a man whom devours life to nothingness
Death,
An immortal new life

Who is to care?
But the innocent, white angels?

58 A Fantasy to Dream

Of colored ducks,
And contemporary reptiles
Raw from the pond of true sanctity

Ballet,
Performed in front of prestigious aristocrats
Tension high
Whilst freedom perished into another Universe
Deep into new dimensions of the unknown

Churches for the fearful to rest their souls
Brought into diverse monarchs of heavens touch
The fearless,
Banished into judgment,
Insecure feeling arise
To the forehead of another pronged soul

A newly woven book,
Read only by one
The creator of the 100th life
Alive in reality,
A place we all dread

A bathtub of sour vinegar
The place a foot is never inserted
The lotus never tricks,
A living soul to lay their time

Peace drawn
In front of memorized Criminals
Bandaged to life's lies
Unseen by crowds of the educated

Praised in several affairs
Lies are seen
As the paper locked in precious bottles
Wrapped in the oceans tender grass

A journey in the skylight of the Amazon
Poison beauty, drawn to starved eyes of passion
When will I surrender,
To a path so delicate?

59 *Nature's Hell*

Of nature's creations
A fine tree of luxury

A black rose
Full of devotion
Brought by men of the dark

A leaf on my pavement
So close to the foot
Yet so far from my consciousness

The winds mind of direction
Self-control,
Leave's no necessity

Insistent powers
Used by scarecrows towards its vile enemy
A black bird knows,
It's time and place
Yet neediness is not to be trusted

An impassionate assurance

To makings of blueberries'
Scrumptious in taste
A disgrace in color

The sound of cherry trees
Vigorous imagination for the Hawk
An immense palace
For a girl of young age

Color in a grey shield
The transparent nature of a green shed
Shone high in everyday needs
Low in priceless morning

The clouds nurture
Evaporated liquids into shapes of laughter
White as heavenly feathers
In days of sunlit paradise
Dark,
In miserable afternoons
Turned to stressful moods
Within humans of work

Birds,
Sing for one another
Their life is existent
When one beak silenced
Another appears

60 Silence Attack

A final path
To magic dust
And darkened shoes

The triumph of a swollen heart
Squeezed by impassionate emotion
Attraction beamed to all corners
The shut off in a soul
The red waste in the body
Spilled in a split of the wrist

The rope hanged on a tall tree
Touched by sacred neck
Pressured upon the senses of one
Tears to land on my all

The words that touched a soul
Woven by weak mind
Spilled by stupid mouths

Affectionate weep of the nemesis
The jealous rage of an attention seeker
Greedy words of a liar

Regretful bluffs of the true

Modern strike to numb ears
A melody of song depressing the timid
Molesting the positivity in innocent face
Attracting unknown creatures to the light

The red vase of creativity
Knocked to the bottom
By the tears of a broken teenager

Resentful love
Bitter taste of insecurity
The notification of worthlessness
Destroyed by words of hatred

Close your eyes
Cover your delicate ears
Listen to your faint voice
Silence will approach you
Silence will attack…

Silence Attack

89

www.ingramcontent.com/pod-product-compliance
Lightning Source LLC
Chambersburg PA
CBHW030905180526
45163CB00004B/1707